Family Life Illustrated
STUDY GUIDE

RONNIE FLOYD

First printing: December 2004

Copyright © 2004 by Ronnie W. Floyd. All rights reserved. No part of this book may be used or reproduced in any manner whatsoever without written permission of the publisher, except in the case of brief quotations in articles and reviews. For information write: New Leaf Press, Inc., P.O. Box 726, Green Forest, AR 72638.

ISBN: 0-89221-599-2
Library of Congress Number: 2004116083

Unless otherwise noted, all scripture references are from the New International Version of the Bible.

Printed in the United States of America

Please visit our website for other great titles:
www.newleafpress.net

For information regarding author interviews,
please contact the publicity department
at (870) 438-5288.

New Leaf Press

Contents

Introduction 5

Women 7

Men 27

Marriage 47

Parenting 67

Finances 89

Teens 101

Introduction

Is the Bible up to date? Can Christians find any principles there that are useful for living in today's society, or are its standards passé?

What's right and what's wrong in today's culture? Are certain things all right for Christian participation because most everybody seems to be doing these things? What about dress styles? Body piercing? Tattoos? Does the Bible say anything about these?

What about money? Is it a sin for Christians to owe money to anyone? Is there anything wrong with driving a new car? Living in a fine home? Does the Bible teach that we should live in poverty?

How should a husband regard his wife, and how should she treat him? What does the Bible have to say about divorce? What about children? What kinds of discipline does the Bible advocate, if any?

God's Word is still very much alive in the 21st century, just as He promised it would be (1 Pet. 1:25). God's Word and His standards have not changed, but the times certainly have. Consequently, many "progressive" Christians have come to believe that God's Word has become outdated and obsolete, simply a collection of stories and morals meant for a first-century Christian, but certainly not applicable to the modern-day Christian.

The "Family Life Illustrated" series is intended as a guide for the Christian to understand the principles of the living Word of God and apply them to his or her life *today*. God says that His Word is still very relevant, even profitable, for today's Christian (1 Tim. 3:16–17).

This study guide is a companion to the series and is intended to be used by an individual or a group in order to more fully comprehend the principles and teaching of the series. This study guide is comprehensive, covering all six titles in the series.

Family Life Illustrated Study Guide

Family Life Illustrated
For WOMEN

YOUR FUTURE: A CHOICE AND A CHALLENGE

7 SECRETS TO SELF-FULFILLMENT

RONNIE FLOYD

Study Guide for WOMEN ILLUSTRATED

Chapter 1
Difficult Times for Christian Women

1. Do you believe that the role of women in today's society is clearly defined? Why or why not?

"I will walk in my house with blameless heart. I will set before my eyes no vile thing" (Ps. 101:2–3).

2. What are some specific influences in your life that sway your thoughts about the role of women in today's society (e.g., magazines, television shows, specific people, etc.)? Briefly state how each affects you, and whether the influence is drawing you toward God or away from God.

"Submit yourselves, then, to God. Resist the devil, and he will flee from you" (James 4:7).

3. Why would the apostle Paul advise the older women to teach the younger women?

"Fix these words of mine in your hearts and minds; tie them as symbols on your hands and bind them on your foreheads. Teach them to your children, talking about them when you sit at home and when you walk along the road, when you lie down and when you get up" (Deut. 11:18–19).

4. List some opportunities you might have in which to mentor a younger Christian woman.

Family Life Illustrated Study Guide

"The mediocre teacher tells. The good teacher explains. The superior teacher demonstrates. The great teacher inspires." – William A. Ward

Chapter 2
Four Things Every Mature Christian Woman Should Do

1. What does Paul mean when he says that the mature women are to be reverent in behavior?

2. What are some practices that can help a woman to be spiritually healthy?

> *"Religion that God our Father accepts as pure and faultless is this: to look after orphans and widows in their distress and to keep oneself from being polluted by the world"* (James 1:27).

3. What is slander, biblically speaking? The word is used to describe whom 34 times in the New Testament?

> *"A fool's mouth is his undoing, and his lips are a snare to his soul"* (Prov. 18:7).

4. What are some things you can do to avoid being a culprit of slander?

> *"The only weapon that becomes sharper with constant use is the tongue."* — Anonymous

FAMILY LIFE ILLUSTRATED STUDY GUIDE

5. Does the Bible teach total abstinence from alcohol? _____ Why is total abstinence from substances such as alcohol recommended for people today?

_____
_____
_____
_____
_____

"Wine is a mocker and beer a brawler; whoever is led astray by them is not wise" (Prov. 20:1).

6. List the four things every Christian woman should do.

1. _____
2. _____
3. _____
4. _____

Chapter 3
Seven Things Every Christian Woman Needs to Know

1. What does it mean to admonish someone?

_____
_____

> *"I myself am convinced, my brothers, that you yourselves are full of goodness, complete in knowledge and competent to instruct one another"* (Rom. 15:14).

2. What is the Greek word that Paul uses for "love," and what kind of love does it imply?

3. Read Romans 12:2. How can the words of this verse help a person to maintain self-control?

> *"The husband should fulfill his marital duty to his wife, and likewise the wife to her husband"* (1 Cor. 7:3).

4. Read 2 Samuel 11:1–12:18 about King David.
a) In the first verse, where should a king have been at this time of year?

b) Instead of being with his army, where was David?

c) Name some of the consequences that came about because David was not in the place where he should have been.

d) What are some "places" named in *Family Life Illustrated: Women,* or other places you can name, of which Christians need to be aware, so we do not fall into temptation such as David?

> *"You may have to fight a battle more than once to win it."*
> — Margaret Thatcher

> *"Drink water from your own cistern, running water from your own well"* (Prov. 5:15).

5. What is the "biblical idea of homemaker"?

6. If a Christian woman is to work outside of the home, what should be her number-one priority (after her relationship with Jesus)?

"Wives, submit to your husbands, as is fitting in the Lord. Husbands, love your wives and do not be harsh with them" (Col. 3:18–19).

7. What happens when a Christian woman refuses to submit to her husband's authority?

_____

_____

8. When is a Christian woman not obligated to submit to her husband's authority?

_____

9. What are some of the dangers of a person saying they are a Christian, but not living by the Word of God?

_____

_____

_____

"Do not merely listen to the word, and so deceive yourselves. Do what it says" (James 1:22).

10. List the seven things every Christian woman should know.

1. _____
2. _____
3. _____
4. _____
5. _____
6. _____
7. _____

FAMILY LIFE ILLUSTRATED STUDY GUIDE

Chapter 4
Mary, Portrait of a Godly Christian Woman

1. Is purity a necessity for today's Christian woman? Why or why not?

2. What comes to mind when you think about purity?

> "Don't let anyone look down on you because you are young, but set an example for the believers in speech, in life, in love, in faith and in purity" (1 Tim. 4:12).

3. What are some things that can influence your ideas about purity?

After a violent storm one night, a large tree, which over the years had become a stately giant, was found lying across the pathway in a park. Nothing but a splintered stump was left. Closer examination showed that is was rotten at the core because thousands of tiny insects had eaten away at its heart. The weakness of that tree was not brought on by the sudden storm; it began the very moment the first insect nested within its bark. With the Holy Spirit's help, let's be very careful to guard our purity. – Our Daily Bread

4. What is the favor of God? Do you think you have found favor with God?

"For the LORD God is a sun and shield; the LORD bestows favor and honor; no good thing does he withhold from those whose walk is blameless" (Ps. 84:11).

Family Life Illustrated Study Guide

5. Read Luke 1:46–55. What do the words of Mary reveal about her character?

> *"Character is what you are in the dark."* — D. L. Moody

6. What does "Too many women today try to find personal esteem in their hobbies" mean?

7. Where should a Christian woman seek esteem?

> *"The lions may grow weak and hungry, but those who seek the Lord lack no good thing"* (Ps. 34:10).

8. In what way was Mary a woman of promise?

9. What are some things you can do each day to become a woman of promise?

_____
_____
_____
_____
_____

> *"Through these he has given us his very great and precious promises, so that through them you may participate in the divine nature and escape the corruption in the world caused by evil desires"* (2 Pet. 1:4).

Chapter 5
A Choice and a Challenge

1. What miracles has God performed in your life?

_____
_____
_____
_____

Family Life Illustrated Study Guide

> *An alcoholic who became a believer was asked how he could possibly believe all the nonsense in the Bible about miracles. "You don't believe that Jesus changed the water into wine do you?"*
>
> *"I sure do, because in our house Jesus changed the whiskey into furniture."*
>
> – R. Stedman, *Authentic Christianity*

2. Is faith necessary for miracles to happen?

3. Define faith in your own words.

> *"Now faith is being sure of what we hope for and certain of what we do not see"* (Heb. 11:1).

4. List the five traits that make Mary a portrait of a godly Christian woman.

1.
2.
3.
4.
5.

5. What is the last thing mentioned that Mary did to help her become a mature Christian woman?

___

___

> *"Within your temple, O God, we meditate on your unfailing love"* (Ps. 48:9).

The Wife of Noble Character

(from Proverbs 31)

A wife of noble character who can find?
She is worth far more than rubies.
Her husband has full confidence in her and lacks nothing of value.
She brings him good, not harm, all the days of her life.
She selects wool and flax and works with eager hands.
She is like the merchant ships, bringing her food from afar.
She gets up while it is still dark; she provides food for her family and portions for her servant girls.
She considers a field and buys it; out of her earnings she plants a vineyard.
She sets about her work vigorously; her arms are strong for her tasks.
She sees that her trading is profitable, and her lamp does not go out at night.

> In her hand she holds the distaff and grasps the spindle with her fingers.
> She opens her arms to the poor and extends her hands to the needy.
> When it snows, she has no fear for her household; for all of them are clothed in scarlet.
> She makes coverings for her bed; she is clothed in fine linen and purple.
> Her husband is respected at the city gate, where he takes his seat among the elders of the land.
> She makes linen garments and sells them, and supplies the merchants with sashes.
> She is clothed with strength and dignity; she can laugh at the days to come.
> She speaks with wisdom, and faithful instruction is on her tongue.
> She watches over the affairs of her household and does not eat the bread of idleness.
> Her children arise and call her blessed; her husband also, and he praises her:
> "Many women do noble things, but you surpass them all."
> Charm is deceptive, and beauty is fleeting; but a woman who fears the LORD is to be praised.
> Give her the reward she has earned, and let her works bring her praise at the city gate.

1. What picture comes to mind when you think of a woman of "noble character"?

_____

_____

_____

_____

> *"And now, my daughter, don't be afraid. I will do for you all you ask. All my fellow townsmen know that you are a woman of noble character"* (Ruth 3:11).

2. Do you picture the woman described in this passage as wealthy? What are some clues that help you to know?

_____
_____
_____

3. Are there any clues in this passage to let us know if she is a happy woman?

_____
_____
_____
_____

4. What are some clues that tell us she is not a selfish person?

_____
_____
_____
_____

> *"Turn my heart toward your statutes and not toward selfish gain"* (Ps. 119:36).

5. What are some clues that she might have a business outside of the home?

_____
_____
_____
_____

Family Life Illustrated Study Guide

6. Are there any clues in the passage about her personal relationship to the Lord? What kind of a relationship do you think she has with Him?

> *"Blessed is the man who does not walk in the counsel of the wicked or stand in the way of sinners or sit in the seat of mockers. But his delight is in the law of the LORD, and on his law he meditates day and night. He is like a tree planted by streams of water, which yields its fruit in season and whose leaf does not wither. Whatever he does prospers"* (Ps. 1:1–3).

Family Life Illustrated Study Guide

Family Life Illustrated
For MEN

WANTED: BATTLEFIELD COMMANDERS LEADING YOUR FAMILY TO VICTORY

7 REASONS MEN MATTER

RONNIE FLOYD

Study Guide for MEN ILLUSTRATED

Chapter 1
Men Are Different from Women

1. Besides obvious physical differences, what are some differences between men and women?

_____
_____
_____
_____
_____
_____
_____

"If a husband is the head of the home, then surely the heart of the home must be the mother." — Anonymous

2. Why do you think God made men and women so different?

_____
_____
_____

"Husbands, love your wives, just as Christ loved the church and gave himself up for her" (Eph. 5:25).

3. Do you think it is important for boys to have an adult male role model and girls to have an adult female role model? Why or why not?

Chapter 2
Jesus, the Man's Man

1. Where did Jesus go immediately after His baptism, and what was the specific purpose that God had in mind?

Family Life Illustrated Study Guide

2. How does the tempting of Jesus in the wilderness help us today according to Hebrews 4:15?

> *"Because he himself suffered when he was tempted, he is able to help those who are being tempted"* (Heb. 2:18).

3. Read the account of the temptation of Christ in Matthew 4:1–11. What did Jesus use to combat Satan with every temptation?

> *"For the word of God is living and active. Sharper than any double-edged sword, it penetrates even to dividing soul and spirit, joints and marrow; it judges the thoughts and attitudes of the heart"* (Heb. 4:12).

4. What should be our weapon when fighting the temptations of Satan?

5. As the Son of God, Jesus had power over the demons in Luke 4:33–37. Do you think we can have the same power over demons today? Read about another exorcism in Mark 9:14–29. What two things (KJV lists two things;

other versions may list only one) does Jesus say a man needs to do to have that kind of power?

_____
_____
_____
_____
_____
_____
_____

> *"If you believe, you will receive whatever you ask for in prayer"* (Matt. 21:22).

6. Jesus spoke in the synagogue at Nazareth at the beginning of His ministry. He read a prophecy about himself from the Book of Isaiah. Read the account in Luke 4:16–21. List the six (KJV lists six; other versions may list only five) prophesied things that Jesus had come to do.

1. _____
2. _____
3. _____
4. _____
5. _____
6. _____

7. In other Scriptures, we can find other things that Jesus, this "man's man," did. Read each Scripture below and write what Jesus did.

Matthew 20:28 _____

Luke 19:10 _____

Family Life Illustrated Study Guide

John 8:29 _____
John 14:31 _____
John 17:4 _____
John 17:6 _____
1 John 3:8 _____

> *"Follow my example, as I follow the example of Christ"*
> (1 Cor. 11:1).

8. Are we able to be the kind of man that Christ exemplified? (See John 14:12 and John 10:4.)

_____
_____
_____
_____

Chapter 3
Why Do We Struggle?

1. Do you picture yourself as the kind of man's man that Jesus was? Why or why not?

_____
_____
_____

2. What does it mean to say "our culture has feminized the male gender"?

"Be men, and fight!" (1 Sam. 4:9).

3. What are some godly traits in a man's character that the secular world seems to be mistaking for a "feminine side"? (Gal. 5:22–23 may help.)

Family Life Illustrated Study Guide

4. In what ways are men forfeiting the future for the immediate?

> *"Character builds slowly, but it can be torn down with incredible swiftness."* — Faith Baldwin

5. Read Ephesians 5:22–6:4. Who should be the spiritual leader of the home?

6. List some things from the "machines, organizations, and fantasies" section or from your own life which hinder a man's spiritual leading of the home.

> *"Therefore, since we are surrounded by such a great cloud of witnesses, let us throw off everything that hinders and the sin that so easily entangles, and let us run with perseverance the race marked out for us"* (Heb. 12:1).

7. Honestly place the following items in order of how they rank in priority in your life. Do the priorities in your life line up with what God would have?

Career	a)
Family	b)
Time spent on yourself	c)
Church	d)
Personal relationship with Christ	e)

8. What does the phrase "get equipped" mean?

_____
_____
_____
_____
_____

9. What things in your own life might you have to give up in order to get equipped?

_____
_____
_____
_____
_____
_____
_____

> *"I am the LORD your God, who brought you out of Egypt, out of the land of slavery. You shall have no other gods before me"* (Exod. 20:2–3).

10. How would you describe who you "really are"?

11. Read 1 Timothy 1:12–17. Did Paul know who he "really was"? How did he identify himself?

"But by the grace of God I am what I am, and his grace to me was not without effect" (1 Cor. 15:10).

12. What is a problem with identifying yourself by what you do?

13. What is a problem with identifying yourself by who you know?

14. What is a problem with identifying yourself by what you own?

> "... a man's life does not consist in the abundance of his possessions" (Luke 12:15).

Chapter 4
Seven Principles for Significance, Part 1

1. What was the significance of God saying to Jeremiah, "Before I formed you in the womb, I knew you"?

Family Life Illustrated Study Guide

> *"I praise you because I am fearfully and wonderfully made; your works are wonderful, I know that full well"* (Ps. 139:14).

2. What events in your own life have shown you that you are important to God?

___

> *"The study of God's word, for the purpose of discovering God's will, is the secret discipline which has formed the greatest characters."* — James W. Alexander

3. What are two important leadership roles for which God has set the man apart?

___

4. What is the one general purpose for which God has chosen man? How do you fulfill this in your life specifically?

___

"Therefore go and make disciples of all nations, baptizing them in the name of the Father and of the Son and of the Holy Spirit, and teaching them to obey everything I have commanded you. And surely I am with you always, to the very end of the age" (Matt. 28:19–20).

5. God did not choose angels for witnessing; He chose man. How have you fulfilled the role of a witness for Christ in your life?

6. What does it mean to have been chosen for God's kingdom?

FAMILY LIFE ILLUSTRATED STUDY GUIDE

Chapter 5
Seven Principles for Significance, Part 2

1. In general, God has chosen us to fulfill the great commission (Matt. 28:19–20). Specifically, how are you fulfilling this obligation?

2. What do you feel is your destiny in God's kingdom?

"Now an angel of the Lord said to Philip, 'Go south to the road — the desert road — that goes down from Jerusalem to Gaza'" (Acts 8:26).

3. Has God touched you? In what way?

4. The text states one reason why God uses us. What is it?

> "*For we know, brothers loved by God, that he has chosen you*" (1 Thess. 1:4).

5. What are some instances where God has used you?

Family Life Illustrated Study Guide

> *"The highest reward for a man's toil is not what he gets for it, but what he becomes by it."* — John Ruskin

6. God has promised to be with you, but does that mean that you will never be opposed?

_____

7. Fill in the blanks in these verses about God's protection for His children from the NIV.

   a) "The name of the LORD is a strong tower; the righteous run to it and are _____" (Prov. 18:10).

   b) "You will be _____, because there is hope; you will look about you and take your rest in _____. You will lie down, with no one to make you _____, and many will court your favor" (Job 11:18–19).

   c) The LORD will keep you from all _____ — he will _____ over your life; the LORD will watch over your _____ and _____ both now and forevermore" (Ps. 121:7–8).

   d) "When you lie down, you will not be _____; when you lie down, your sleep will be _____" (Prov. 3:24).

   e) "The LORD is my _____ and my salvation — whom shall I _____? The LORD is the _____ of my life — of whom shall I be _____?" (Ps. 27:1).

Chapter 6
Wanted : Battlefield Commanders

1. If we are battlefield commanders, who is the captain of our army?

    _____

2. Who are we fighting?

    _____

> *"I give you this instruction in keeping with the prophecies once made about you, so that by following them you may fight the good fight"* (1 Tim. 1:18).

3. What are the three characteristics of a godly battlefield commander?
   a) _____
   b) _____
   c) _____

4. What things in your life are you most committed to?

    _____
    _____
    _____
    _____

Family Life Illustrated Study Guide

> *"I want to know Christ and the power of his resurrection and the fellowship of sharing in his sufferings, becoming like him in his death, and so, somehow, to attain to the resurrection from the dead"* (Phil. 3:10–11).

5. What does it mean to say, "The standard of Christ is His cross"?

> *"One machine can do the work of fifty ordinary men. No machine can do the work of one extraordinary man."* — Elbert Hubbard

Family Life Illustrated Study Guide

Family Life Illustrated
for MARRIAGE

WHAT'S MISSING IN YOUR RELATIONSHIP...

Sealed with a Kiss:
8 STAGES OF ROMANCE

RONNIE FLOYD

Study Guide for
MARRIAGE ILLUSTRATED

Chapter 1
The Revelation of Marriage

1. Who designed marriage?

2. Who were the first married couple?

"Marriage is like twirling a baton, turning handsprings or eating with chopsticks. It looks easy until you try it." — Helen Rowland

3. What does marriage have to do with family?

4. What does family have to do with the kingdom of God?

5. In light of the last questions, how important is marriage?

"Try praising your wife, even if it does frighten her at first."
— Billy Sunday

6. Marriage was ordained by God from the beginning. It was established by God's Word. Considering this, should only Christians be married? Going one step further, do you think the laws of God's Word apply only to Christians? Why or why not?

FAMILY LIFE ILLUSTRATED STUDY GUIDE

7. Why, in your opinion, would homosexuals want to marry?

8. If a couple is married by a justice of the peace instead of a minister, does God still recognize that marriage? See Romans 13:1 to help you answer.

> *A couple married for 15 years began having more than usual disagreements. They wanted to make their marriage work and agreed on an idea the wife had. For one month they planned to drop a slip in a "Fault" box. The boxes would provide a place to let the other know about daily irritations. The wife was diligent in her efforts and approach: "leaving the jelly top off the jar," "Wet towels on the shower floor," "Dirty socks not in hamper," on and on until the end of the month. After dinner, at the end of the month, they exchanged boxes. The husband reflected on what he had done wrong. Then the wife opened her box and began reading. They were all the same, the message on each slip was, "I love you!"*
> — Source Unknown

9. Besides the physical "oneness" of a married couple, in what other ways do the two become as one?

10. God intended for marriage to be permanent. How important is it for Christians to marry other Christians, and why?

> *"Do not be yoked together with unbelievers. For what do righteousness and wickedness have in common? Or what fellowship can light have with darkness?"* (2 Cor. 6:14).

11. What are some things a Christian should look for in finding a spouse?

Family Life Illustrated Study Guide

_____
_____
_____
_____

12. What are the three characteristics of marriage?

a) _____

b) _____

c) _____

> *"For this reason a man will leave his father and mother and be united to his wife, and the two will become one flesh"* (Eph. 5:31).

Chapter 2
Three Characteristics of a Healthy Marriage

1. If you are married, do you remember any of your wedding vows? If you are not married, what vows do you think you would like to make at your wedding?

_____
_____
_____
_____

2. What is one huge reason why marriages fail?

> *Astronaut Michael Collins, speaking at a banquet, quoted the estimate that the average man speaks 25,000 words a day and the average woman 30,000. Then he added: "Unfortunately, when I come home each day I've spoken my 25,000 — and my wife hasn't started her 30,000."*
>
> — Sports Illustrated

3. In your own words, what is commitment?

4. If you're married, do you have much rejoicing in your marriage? What can you do to have a more joyful marriage?

Family Life Illustrated Study Guide

"Enjoy life with your wife, whom you love" (Eccles. 9:9).

5. If you're married, what are some things that attract you to your spouse?

6. How many times a day do you tell your spouse "I love you"?

7. What are some ways you can show your spouse that you love him or her?

Chapter 3
Communication: Turning a Problem into a Blessing

1. "The average working business professional spends, on average, just two minutes per day in meaningful communication with their spouse." Do you agree or disagree? If you're married, about how many minutes a day would you be able to say you spend in meaningful communication with your spouse?

_____
_____
_____
_____

2. Can you remember any recent events in your life where you placed the value of things over other people?

_____
_____
_____
_____
_____
_____

"Love people and use things — not the other way around."
— Anonymous

FAMILY LIFE ILLUSTRATED STUDY GUIDE

3. When are the best times of the day for communication with your spouse? With your children? As a family?

_____
_____
_____
_____
_____
_____

> *"Let your conversation be always full of grace, seasoned with salt, so that you may know how to answer everyone"* (Col. 4:6).

4. What does listening to another person tell him or her?

_____
_____

> *"In your anger do not sin: Do not let the sun go down while you are still angry, and do not give the devil a foothold"* (Eph. 4:26–27).

5. Who is the greatest adversary of fine communication, and why would he want to cause confusion between a husband and wife?

_____
_____
_____
_____
_____

6. Doesn't it make sense why Satan is on the rampage against families? God ordained marriage and family to be the perpetuators of the gospel. Families are the foundation of a godly nation. When the family falls apart, the nation falls apart. Do you agree or disagree?

_____
_____
_____
_____
_____
_____

7. Are your words harsher when responding to spouse and family members than non-family contacts? If so, what can be done to be more amiable toward your family?

_____
_____
_____
_____

> "Wives, submit to your husbands, as is fitting in the Lord. Husbands, love your wives and do not be harsh with them" (Col. 3:18–19).

8. How can you learn to speak wisely?

_____
_____
_____

Family Life Illustrated Study Guide

9. What are the three goals of communication?

a) _____

b) _____

c) _____

> *The speaker at our woman's club was lecturing on marriage and asked the audience how many of us wanted to "mother" our husbands. One member in the back row raised her hand.*
> *"You do want to mother your husband?" the speaker asked.*
> *"Mother?" the woman echoed. "I thought you said smother."*
> — Reader's Digest, October 1993

10. In Ephesians 4:29, what are some synonyms for the word "corrupt"?

_____

_____

_____

_____

11. List the 4:32 Rules from Ephesians 4:32.

a) _____

b) _____

c) _____

> *"A word aptly spoken is like apples of gold in settings of silver"* (Prov. 25:11).

Chapter 4
How Do We Decide?

1. How can you tell if you were led to a major decision of your life by God?

2. When discerning God's will concerning a decision, what must you ask yourselves?

"Multitudes, multitudes in the valley of decision!" (Joel 3:14).

3. What must you remember about timing?

4. When working through a decision, which passage of Scripture should you use, and what are some of the questions that you should ask yourself?

> *A husband and wife, prior to marriage, decided that he'd make all the major decisions and she the minor ones. After 20 years of marriage, he was asked how this arrangement had worked. "Great! In all these years I've never had to make a major decision."*
>
> — Source unknown

5. What should you ask yourself about the decision concerning the fruit of the Spirit?

> *"But the fruit of the Spirit is love, joy, peace, patience, kindness, goodness, faithfulness, gentleness and self-control"* (Gal. 5:22–23).

6. Everything that you do in your life should do what?

7. God works in the lives of His children for a purpose. With this in mind, what is the last question of the decision-making process?

8. Have you made any important decisions recently? Do you feel that you followed God in making those decisions? How did they turn out?

"Trust in the LORD with all your heart and lean not on your own understanding; in all your ways acknowledge him, and he will make your paths straight" (Prov. 3:5–6).

Chapter 5
Turn Up the Romance

1. What does it mean to "affirm" your spouse?

2. Give some examples of things you can say to affirm your spouse.

Family Life Illustrated Study Guide

> *"There is no more lovely, friendly, and charming relationship, communion, or company than a good marriage."*
> — Martin Luther

3. What follows affirmation?

4. What are some signs that your spouse is attracted to you?

5. Finish this statement, "If your girlfriend or boyfriend isn't faithful to you in your courtship...."

> *"Houses and wealth are inherited from parents, but a prudent wife is from the LORD"* (Prov. 19:14).

6. What does the text mean by the term "initiation"?

> *I am the wife of a Baptist minister and have seen many marriage licenses. On one, after the blank for number of marriages, the groom had answered: "First." The bride had entered the word: "Last."*
>
> – Reader's Digest

7. Should the affirmation, attraction, and initiation stop after the wedding?

> *"My lover spoke and said to me, 'Arise, my darling, my beautiful one, and come with me' "* (Song of Sol. 2:10).

8. What three things could the term "sister" mean in the ancient near-eastern culture?

a)
b)
c)

9. Does the Bible encourage sexual intimacy between a husband and wife?

> *"My lover is mine and I am his; he browses among the lilies"* (Song of Sol. 2:16).

10. How would you rate your marriage on a scale of 1 to 10, with 10 being the best? What are some things you have learned from this book that you can implement to improve your marriage?

FAMILY LIFE ILLUSTRATED STUDY GUIDE

"The husband should fulfill his marital duty to his wife, and likewise the wife to her husband. The wife's body does not belong to her alone but also to her husband. In the same way, the husband's body does not belong to him alone but also to his wife. Do not deprive each other except by mutual consent and for a time, so that you may devote yourselves to prayer" (1 Cor. 7:3–5).

MARRIAGE

Family Life Illustrated Study Guide

Family Life Illustrated
for PARENTS

ONE LESSON EVERY CHILD MUST BE TAUGHT

NEW!
SECRET SUCCESS FOR THE DISCIPLINE WARS

RONNIE FLOYD

Study Guide for
PARENTING ILLUSTRATED

Chapter 1
A Tough but Rewarding Job

1. Read Genesis 1:26–28. What was God's first command to man?

2. Before she was visited by an angel, Samson's mother was barren. Can you name any other women in the Bible who were barren until God blessed them with children? (See Gen. 11:30, 25:21, 29:31; 1 Sam. 1:5; Luke 1:7.)

3. Using the mothers from question 2, name each one's son who ended her barrenness, and tell how that son was used of God.

> *Owen Wister, an old college friend of Theodore Roosevelt, was visiting him at the White House. Roosevelt's daughter Alice kept running in and out of the room until Wister finally asked if there wasn't something Roosevelt could do to control her.*
>
> *"Well," said the president, "I can do one of two things. I can be president of the United States or I can control Alice. I cannot possibly do both."*
>
> – Bits & Pieces

4. Do you think in each case that the barrenness was for a purpose? What would seem to be the purpose for barrenness in the Bible?

5. What unusual request did Manoah and his wife ask of God when they found out they were going to be parents?

6. What is cited as the "one major and overriding responsibility as parents"?

Family Life Illustrated Study Guide

"O my people, hear my teaching; listen to the words of my mouth. I will open my mouth in parables, I will utter hidden things, things from of old — what we have heard and known, what our fathers have told us. We will not hide them from their children; we will tell the next generation the praiseworthy deeds of the Lord, his power, and the wonders he has done. He decreed statutes for Jacob and established the law in Israel, which he commanded our forefathers to teach their children, so the next generation would know them, even the children yet to be born, and they in turn would tell their children. Then they would put their trust in God and would not forget his deeds but would keep his commands. They would not be like their forefathers — a stubborn and rebellious generation, whose hearts were not loyal to God, whose spirits were not faithful to him" (Ps. 78:1–8).

7. Write what each letter of the acronym MODEL stands for.

M _____

O _____

D _____

E _____

L _____

Chapter 2
Move Your Children to God

1. Deuteronomy 6:5 declares "You shall love the Lord your God with all your _____, with all your _____, and with all your _____.

2. Tell what each of the three things answered in question 1 means:

a) _____

b) _____

c) _____

3. Before you can expect your children to wholly follow God, what must you do?

_____

_____

> *An author for* Reader's Digest *writes how he studied the Amish people in preparation for an article on them. In his observation at the school yard, he noted that the children never screamed or yelled. This amazed him. He spoke to the schoolmaster. He remarked how he had not once heard an Amish child yell, and asked why the schoolmaster thought that was so. The schoolmaster replied, "Well, have you ever heard an Amish adult yell?"*
> — Reader's Digest

4. What does Deuteronomy 6:7 tell us about when and where to teach our children?

_____

_____

5. How often do you talk about the Lord to your children? Is His name a household name in your home?

_____

_____

_____

Family Life Illustrated Study Guide

"Having children makes you no more a parent than having a piano makes you a pianist." — Michael Levine

6. What reminders of the law were employed by the Old Testament Jews?

7. What are four things you do to nurture your children's relationship with Christ?

8. Do you pray with your children? When is a good time to pray with them?

"I learned the idea of Quality Time was an evil lie. Some experts pushed the idea that successful overachievers, those we call Yuppies today, could have children and be guilt-free about the little time they were able to devote to them. The remedy was Quality Time. Sort of like one-minute parenting. It went like this: Be sure to make what little time you are able to spend with your child Quality Time. What garbage. I've seen the results of kids who were given only Quality Time. The problem is that kids don't know the difference. What they need is time — all they can get. Quantity time is quality time, whether you're discussing the meaning of the cosmos or just climbing on dad." — Jerry Jenkins, *Hedges*

9. Do you have a quiet time? When?

_____

_____

_____

10. Do you have a family devotion time? How often?

_____

_____

_____

"The Christian home is the Master's workshop where the process of character molding is silently, lovingly, faithfully, and successfully carried on." — Richard Monckton Milnes

11. How strict are you in regarding the Sabbath? Do you often miss church in favor of leisurely activities? Read Isaiah 58:13–14 regarding God's promise for keeping the Sabbath holy. How do you measure up?

_____

_____

_____

Family Life Illustrated Study Guide

12. Read 2 Samuel 13:1–18. What did Amnon want?

13. Who was Amnon's friend?

14. How influential in the life of Amnon was his friend?

15. Do you know who your children's friends are? Do you think that you should be a strong influence in helping your children choose the right friends?

> "Could I climb to the highest places in Athens, I would lift up my voice and proclaim; Fellow citizens, why do you turn and scrape every stone to gather wealth, and take so little care of the children to whom you must someday relinquish it all?" — Socrates

16. Do you think it is easier to be saved at a younger age or at an older age? Why?

_____

_____

_____

Nineteenth century Scottish preacher Horatius Bonar asked 253 Christian friends at what ages they were converted. Here's what he discovered:

> *Under 20 years of age — 138*
> *Between 20 and 30 — 85*
> *Between 30 and 40 — 22*
> *Between 40 and 50 — 4*
> *Between 50 and 60 — 3*
> *Between 60 and 70 — 1*
> *Over 70 — 0*
>
> *— From Daily Bread*

Chapter 3
Open Your Heart

1. What, as a parent, can you learn from Paul's admonition of the Corinthian church in 2 Corinthians 6?

_____

_____

FAMILY LIFE ILLUSTRATED STUDY GUIDE

2. What one important thing can you do to help your child know that you are really listening?

> *"My dear brothers, take note of this: Everyone should be quick to listen, slow to speak, and slow to become angry"* (James 1:19).

3. Why is it important to create a bridge of trust and openness with your children while they are young?

> *"Often parents say 'no' only because it simplifies matters. I've made a practice of saying 'yes' when the consequences are not far-reaching. Then the important 'no's' are considerably easier for teens to accept. Think about why 'no' is best, and back up your decision with a logical reason."* — Sally Stuart

4. What's the best way to have an open heart toward your child?

"He who loves a pure heart and whose speech is gracious will have the king for his friend" (Prov. 22:11).

5. "Teachable moments" are the best times to teach your child, but do you spend enough time with your child to find those moments? How can you arrange your schedule so you can spend more time with your child?

_____
_____
_____
_____
_____

Chapter 4
Discipline Your Children

1. What do the Hebrew and Greek words translated as "discipline" usually mean?

_____
_____
_____
_____

"Blessed is the man whom God corrects; so do not despise the discipline of the Almighty" (Job 5:17).

2. Read Hebrews 12:5–11. What does it mean to receive discipline from the Lord?

3. Should we feel the same way about the discipline of our own child?

> "All Scripture is God-breathed and is useful for teaching, rebuking, correcting, and training in righteousness, so that the man of God may be thoroughly equipped for every good work" (2 Tim. 3:16–17).

4. What should be the basis for all of the authority in our home?

5. No one is without a higher authority. Read Romans 13:1–7 and write down some principles from God's Word about authority.

> *"The job of a football coach is to make men do what they don't want to do, in order to achieve what they've always wanted to be."* — Tom Landry

6. Children need rules and boundaries and should be corrected when they exceed these. Do you agree? Why or why not?

_____
_____
_____
_____
_____

> *"If they obey and serve him, they will spend the rest of their days in prosperity and their years in contentment"* (Job 36:11).

7. Biblical discipline is always done in _____.

> *"Be completely humble and gentle; be patient, bearing with one another in love"* (Eph. 4:2).

8. What does Ephesians 6:4 warn fathers about, regarding discipline?

_____
_____

9. Does the Bible teach that physical correction is sometimes necessary? Is this "abuse"?

_____
_____

Family Life Illustrated Study Guide

_____
_____
_____
_____
_____

"Folly is bound up in the heart of a child, but the rod of discipline will drive it far from him" (Prov. 22:15).

10. What should you teach your child as best preventative measure for peer pressure?
_____
_____

11. Another good discipline to teach your child is to _____
_____.

"I have hidden your word in my heart that I might not sin against you" (Ps. 119:11).

Chapter 5
Eliminate All Unnecessary Stuff

1. What is the number one idol today, even among Christians?
_____
_____

> *"I am the LORD your God, who brought you out of Egypt, out of the land of slavery. You shall have no other gods before me"* (Exod. 20:2–3).

2. What did Jesus mean when He said that we are to hate our families if we are to be His disciples?

___

3. What did the cross literally mean to first-century Christians? What does it mean to us today?

___

> *"May I never boast except in the cross of our Lord Jesus Christ, through which the world has been crucified to me, and I to the world"* (Gal. 6:14).

4. For you, what has it cost to follow Christ?

Family Life Illustrated Study Guide

5. What are some things in your life that you have had to forsake or need to forsake in order to walk closer to Christ?

> *"Suppose one of you wants to build a tower. Will he not first sit down and estimate the cost to see if he has enough money to complete it?"* (Luke 14:28).

6. In what ways can Christians be compared to salt?

"Is tasteless food eaten without salt, or is there flavor in the white of an egg? I refuse to touch it; such food makes me ill" (Job 6:6–7).

7. What is the lesson that we can learn from the account of Dagon and the ark of the covenant?

___

___

___

___

Chapter 6
Love Them Unconditionally

1. How often should we tell and show our children that we love them?

___

___

2. Has there been a situation in which your child has gone in a direction against your wishes, or gone in an ungodly direction? How did you handle it, and what was the outcome?

___

___

Family Life Illustrated Study Guide

_____
_____
_____
_____

> *"I will set out and go back to my father and say to him: Father, I have sinned against heaven and against you. I am no longer worthy to be called your son; make me like one of your hired men. So he got up and went to his father"* (Luke 15:18–20).

3. "Prodigals have a way of _____."

4. The spoken word can build character and reinforce learned values, but it can also be destructive and tear down a person's confidence. Do you agree? Why or why not?

_____
_____
_____
_____
_____

> One parent, tired of reading bedtime stories to his daughter, decided to record several of her favorite stories on tape. He told her, "Now you can hear your stories anytime you want. Isn't that great?"
>
> She looked at the machine for a moment and then replied, "No. It hasn't got a lap."
>
> — Source unknown

5. If you do not already, would you be willing to commit to praying and fasting for your child?

> *"I prayed for this child, and the L*ORD* has granted me what I asked of him"* (1 Sam. 1:27).

6. Is your family involved in a local church? What are some things about the church that you like and appreciate?

7. What are some things about the church that you do not like?

Family Life Illustrated Study Guide

> *"And I tell you that you are Peter, and on this rock I will build my church, and the gates of Hades will not overcome it"* (Matt. 16:18).

8. To whom should you NOT voice your complaints about the church? To whom should you speak about your dislikes?

9. Is it possible for you to love your child unconditionally?

Afterword
The Only Perfect Parent

1. Who is the only perfect parent?

2. "A godly home is no guarantee of a _____."

> *"Children are natural mimics: they act like their parents in spite of every attempt to teach them good manners."* — Anonymous

3. Write Proverbs 23:24 below in your own words.

_____
_____
_____
_____
_____
_____
_____
_____

FAMILY LIFE ILLUSTRATED STUDY GUIDE

Family Life Illustrated
For FINANCES

ROBBED! YOUR FUTURE SAVINGS

On Firm Footing — **OVERCOMING DEBT AND CREDIT WOES**

RONNIE FLOYD

Study Guide for
FINANCES ILLUSTRATED

Chapter 1
The Facts about Money

1. The Bible shows us that there is truly "nothing new under the sun," including money problems. Read Proverbs 31, and Ecclesiastes 2; compare and contrast the business principles and motives for earning.

2. What was Solomon's conclusion about lifelong efforts to earn more and more money?

3. The word "vanity" is used 37 times in the Book of Ecclesiastes. What is the meaning of the word, as used here?

"Money can buy the husk of many things, but not the kernel. It brings you food, but not appetite; medicine, but not health; acquaintances, but not friends; servants, but not faithfulness; days of joy, but not peace and happiness." — Henrik Ibsen

4. What result of Solomon's quest for wealth left him in a reflective mood at the end of his life?

5. What is the great danger of money, according to the apostle Paul?

6. What are the seven facts about money that everyone needs to know?

"Then I realized that it is good and proper for a man to eat and drink, and to find satisfaction in his toilsome labor under the sun during the few days of life God has given him — for this is his lot. Moreover, when God gives any man wealth and possessions, and

FAMILY LIFE ILLUSTRATED STUDY GUIDE

enables him to enjoy them, to accept his lot and be happy in his work — this is a gift from God. He seldom reflects on the days of his life, because God keeps him occupied with gladness of heart" (Eccles. 5:18–20).

Chapter 2
A Sobering Evaluation

1. In what way will each believer be held accountable to Christ?

2. What three areas of evaluation must each of us prepare for?

3. First Corinthians 3 tells us two ways we can build our lives. What are they, and which one lasts?

"Money is a good servant, but a dangerous master."
— Dominique Bouhours

4. What crucial question must we all answer, regarding what we've done with what we have?

___

Chapter 4
Financial Enemies of the Family

1. In addition to cultural factors, the modern family is under attack through finances. List the seven "enemies" of families, financially speaking.

___

2. What does Luke 12 tell us about being wealthy, as opposed to being wealthy in God?

Family Life Illustrated Study Guide

3. What percentage of Americans know how to balance a checkbook?

4. List three statistics concerning credit card debt, then discuss potential implications for both a family and a single person who accumulate credit card debt.

"Without debt, without care." — Italian proverb

5. Is your family within an acceptable range for credit card debt? List three ways you can reduce your debt.

6. What does the Bible say about "get-rich-quick" schemes?

Chapter 4
A Six-Step Formula for Financial Health

1. What or who is your ultimate financial authority?

2. Is tithing commanded? Do you tithe a percentage of your income?

3. In Matthew 6, what two things destroy wealth?

4. Which three steps to financial freedom does your family do well?

Family Life Illustrated Study Guide

5. Which three steps are a struggle?

> *"When I have any money, I get rid of it as quickly as possible, lest it find a way into my heart."* — John Wesley

6. Do you think of giving as a sacrifice, or as an investment?

7. Which 18th century Englishman made it a habit to give away money? What resulted?

8. What is the "secret" or outline for a secure financial plan, as set out in 1 Chronicles 29:3?

Chapter 5
What's in Your Hand?

1. Moses was raised in the wealth and splendor of ancient Egypt, but when God called him to help His people, what main thing did God ask him?

_____
_____
_____

2. Do you remember a time when God gave you the means to accomplish some task, but you passed it by? How did you feel?

_____
_____
_____
_____
_____

3. List a time in your life when you did answer God's call. What assets did you use to accomplish the plan He had for you?

_____
_____
_____
_____

for Finances | 97

FAMILY LIFE ILLUSTRATED STUDY GUIDE

4. We're often told that finances cause many marriages to struggle. Of the two groups — marrieds and singles — who struggles more with money and why?

Family Life Illustrated
For TEENS

SEX WHEN, WHERE, & IF

**PLUS:
LIFE IN A CAGE**
Discover Keys to Your Future

RONNIE FLOYD

Study Guide for
TEENS ILLUSTRATED

Chapter 1
The Most Important Decision You'll Ever Make

1. What would you consider your most important decision made to date?

2. What does it mean to be a Christian?

3. What is an important factor in developing a relationship with Jesus Christ?

"Above all, you must understand that no prophecy of Scripture came about by the prophet's own interpretation. For prophecy never had its origin in the will of man, but men spoke from God as they were carried along by the Holy Spirit"
(2 Peter 1:19–20).

4. What are four reasons we should treat the Bible seriously?

5. Paul said that the Bible is _____

_____ (2 Tim. 3:16–17).

How can these concepts impact your daily life?

Family Life Illustrated Study Guide

"Young people do the impossible before they find out it's impossible — that's why God uses them so often." — Loren Cunningham

6. Is it important to attend a church and be active in it?

___
___

Chapter 2
How to Live a Long Time

1. Discuss Exodus 20:12. Have you successfully applied its message in your life? Why or why not?

___
___
___
___

2. What does the Greek word for *obey* mean?

___
___

3. Are there exceptions to being obedient to your parents? Discuss.

___
___
___
___

4. What does it mean to leave and cleave?

"There are no shortcuts to spiritual maturity. It takes time to be holy." — Erwin Lutzer

Chapter 3
Why Are You Here?

1. Do you believe that you have a unique mission in life?

2. What is the key to discovering your life mission?

FAMILY LIFE ILLUSTRATED STUDY GUIDE

3. Have you discussed with someone what your life's mission might be? Discuss several important factors in determining your purpose.

Chapter 4
Real Life Begins Now

1. What is the real purpose of education?

2. List six things crucial to learning:

3. In the past, the word vocation meant something different. Compare and contrast the former meaning with today's:

_____
_____
_____

4. Former U.S. presidents U.S. Grant and Harry Truman tried many vocations before they found their true calling, respectively. Grant helped turn the tide of the Civil War, while Truman led his country through another dark war. How many people do you know who were apparent "failures" in life, but came back to do something great for God?

_____
_____
_____
_____
_____

Chapter 5
Get Real

1. If you've lost your virginity, what is the first thing you can do to restore right relationships?

_____
_____

FAMILY LIFE ILLUSTRATED STUDY GUIDE

2. What are several practical suggestions for maintaining your purity?

_____
_____
_____
_____
_____
_____

3. What is the great secret to remaining a virgin?

_____
_____
_____

Chapter 6
Change Is Hard

1. What did God promise Joshua as he began to lead the Israelites? How can this apply to your life?

_____
_____
_____

2. What does Ephesians 3:20 say about God's commitment to us in times of trouble?

_____

_____

_____

_____

> *"If we try to resist loss and change or to hold on to blessings and joy belonging to a past which must drop away from us, we postpone all the blessings awaiting us on a higher level and find ourselves left in a barren, bleak winter of sorrow and loneliness."*
> — Hannah Hurnard

Also by Dr. Ronnie Floyd...

ISBN 0-89221-583-6

Are you happening to life or is life simply happening to you? Overwhelmed, overworked, stressed, and tired, it's easy to lose sight of things important to you as a woman, wife, and perhaps even a mother. Be empowered, be decisive, and be open to God's gently guiding hand in your life! God can be what you need – He can strengthen, calm, and sustain you when life seems impossible. No matter what you face, God can give you the knowledge and wisdom to adapt, endure, and affect a change!

Available at Christian bookstores nationwide.

Also by Dr. Ronnie Floyd . . .

ISBN 0-89221-586-0

It seems like everything keeps changing and no one understands. Every day seems to bring more pivotal decisions to be made. Life is complicated and stressful, and you feel you are alone! Fight the isolation – don't be a spectator in your own life! Get powerful solutions and strategies to survive and thrive during the toughest time of your life – and find out how to rely on God when life overwhelms you!

Available at Christian bookstores nationwide.

Also by Dr. Ronnie Floyd . . .

Family Life Illustrated for PARENTS

ONE LESSON EVERY CHILD MUST BE TAUGHT

NEW! SECRET SUCCESS FOR THE DISCIPLINE WARS

RONNIE FLOYD

ISBN 0-89221-588-7

Your job, your finances, your friends — nothing you ever do will matter as much as being a good parent to your child. Going beyond the surface strategies and quick psychobabble solutions, this book reveals solid, God-based insight on becoming a more effective parent. Don't choose to struggle alone — tap into the wealth of wisdom God wants to share with you and find how you can make a positive, remarkable, and lasting change in the lives of your children today!

Available at Christian bookstores nationwide.

Also by Dr. Ronnie Floyd . . .

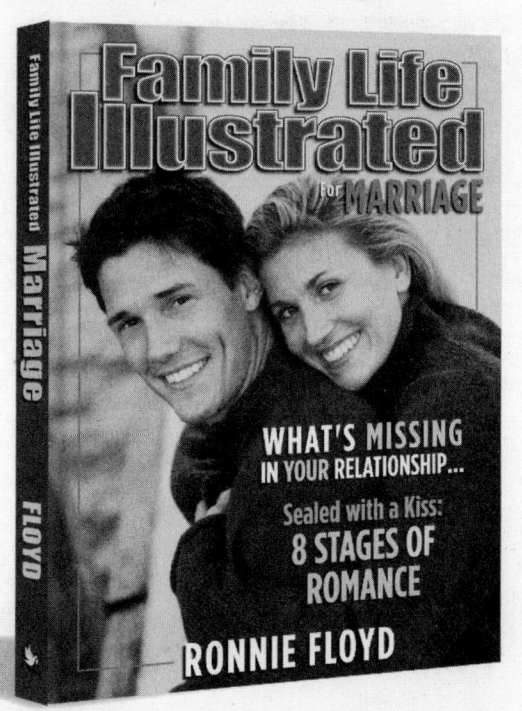

ISBN 0-89221-585-2

    Thought about your marriage lately? Or do you just take it for granted? Marriage is not a passive enterprise — it takes skill, work, and attention if you want it to survive in the "disposable" culture of our society today. Do you have the marriage God wants you to have? Tired of going through the motions, feeling helpless to make the change for the better you know you need to make? It's time to take control and make your marriage be the true partnership that God designed. Don't wait to make a renewed commitment for marital success!

Available at Christian bookstores nationwide.

Also by Dr. Ronnie Floyd . . .

ISBN 0-89221-584-4

Are you sitting on the sidelines of your family's life? Investing in material goods instead of Christ-like character? You need to make a difference, be a part of, and a leader for your spouse and your children. God is looking for men willing to fight for the future of their families — and be examples of strong Christian leadership within their communities. Don't be irrelevant! Be a God-inspired guide for your family each day!

Available at Christian bookstores nationwide.

Also by Dr. Ronnie Floyd . . .

ISBN 0-89221-587-9

    Money, debt, credit card complications — believe it or not, the Bible can be the most practical guide to financial management you will ever find! Simple, easy-to-implement solutions don't require high cost solutions or painful personal concessions. Don't do without the answers which can help change your financial future and solve a critical area of stress affecting you, your family, or even your marriage. Invest in God's wisdom, and reap the blessings He has in store for you!

Available at Christian bookstores nationwide.

About the Author...

Recognizing the vital importance of the family in the success of not only individuals, but for our society today, the "Family Life Illustrated" series offers real answers for real-life problems being faced each day by families. Articulate, informative, and always relevant — Dr. Ronnie Floyd is reaching the hearts of millions weekly through his broadcast ministry Invitation to Life, aired on WGN's Superstation and other television networks nationally each week. An accomplished author of 17 books as well as a powerful group speaker, Dr. Floyd has over 27 years of ministry experience and is senior pastor for a congregation of 15,000 in Northwest Arkansas. Dr. Floyd has been been seen on Fox News, WorldNetDaily, Janet Parshall's America, Washington Watch, USA Radio Network, FamilyNet, and more!

MORE RESOURCES FROM DR. RONNIE W. FLOYD

CD/VHS/DVD
"Family Life Illustrated Series"

CD/VHS/DVD
"The Gay Agenda"

Other Books By Dr. Floyd
Life on Fire
How to Pray
The Power of Prayer and Fasting
The Meaning of a Man

Weekly International Television and Internet

Sundays: (7:30 a.m. CST) WGN SUPERSTATION

Thursdays: (9:00 p.m. CST) Daystar Christian Television Network

Sundays: (9:15 a.m. CST) Live webcast on
www.fbcspringdale.org

For more information on all resources: www.invitationtolife.org

For information about our church:
www.fbcspringdale.org   www.churchph.com

or call (479) 751-4523 and ask for Invitation to Life